RACIAL JUSTICE IN AMERICA
INDIGENOUS PE

What Is
LAND BACK?

HEATHER BRUEGL

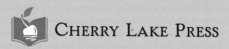
CHERRY LAKE PRESS

Published in the United States of America by Cherry Lake Publishing Group
Ann Arbor, Michigan
www.cherrylakepublishing.com

Reading Adviser: Beth Walker Gambro, MS, Ed., Reading Consultant, Yorkville, IL
Cover Art: Felicia Macheske

Produced by Focus Strategic Communications Inc.

Photo Credits: © Rena Schild/Shutterstock, 5; © Steve Sanchez Photos/Shutterstock, 7; © ASSOCIATED PRESS, 9, 26, 27, 29, 30;
© melissamn/Shutterstock, 10; United States Department of the Interior, Public domain, 13; © piemags/DCM/Alamy Stock
Photo, 15; Treaty with the Sioux-Brule, Oglala, Miniconjou, Yanktonai, Hunkpapa, Blackfeet, Cuthead, Two Kettle, San Arcs, and
Santee-and Arapaho, 4/29/1868, General Records of the United States Government, Record Group 11, National Archives, 19;
David F. Barry, Photographer, Bismarck, Dakota Territory, Public domain, via Wikimedia Commons, 21; © Chad Davis/Flickr CC
BY-NC 2.0 DEED, 22; Burton Historical Collection, Detroit Public Library, Unknown author, Photo edited by User:PawełMM, Public
domain, via Wikimedia Commons, 23; The White House from Washington, D.C., Public domain, via Wikimedia Commons, 25;
Derek Simeone, CC BY 2.0 via Wikimedia Commons, 28

Cherry Lake Press is an imprint of Cherry Lake Publishing Group.

Library of Congress Cataloging-in-Publication Data

Names: Bruegl, Heather, author.
Title: What is Land Back? / by Heather Bruegl, Oneida Nation of Wisconsin/Stockbridge-Munsee.
Description: Ann Arbor, Michigan : Cherry Lake Publishing, [2024]. | Series: Racial justice in America: Indigenous peoples |
    Audience: Grades 7-9 | Summary: "The Land Back movement is an ongoing political and social Indigenous movement.
    Readers will learn about what this movement is all about and the work that is being done to empower Indigenous peoples
    across the United States. The Racial Justice in America: Indigenous Peoples series explores the issues specific to the
    Indigenous communities in the United States in a comprehensive, honest, and age-appropriate way. This series was written
    by Indigenous historian and public scholar Heather Bruegl, a citizen of the Oneida Nation of Wisconsin and a first-line
    descendent Stockbridge Munsee. The series was developed to reach children of all races and encourage them to approach
    race, diversity, and inclusion with open eyes and minds"– Provided by publisher.
Identifiers: LCCN 2023043605 | ISBN 9781668937990 (hardcover) | ISBN 9781668939031 (paperback) |
    ISBN 9781668940372 (ebook) | ISBN 9781668941720 (pdf)
Subjects: LCSH: Indians of North America–Land tenure–United States–Juvenile literature. | Indians of North America–
    Reparations–Juvenile literature. | Activism–Juvenile literature.
Classification: LCC E98.L3 B78 2024 | DDC 333.3/173—dc23/eng/20231018
LC record available at https://lccn.loc.gov/2023043605

Cherry Lake Publishing would like to acknowledge the work of the Partnership for 21st Century Learning, a Network of
Battelle for Kids. Please visit Battelle for Kids online for more information.

Printed in the United States of America

Note from publisher: Websites change regularly, and their future contents are outside of our control. Supervise children
when conducting any recommended online searches for extended learning opportunities.

Heather Bruegl, Oneida Nation of Wisconsin/Stockbridge-Munsee is a Madonna University graduate
with a Master of Arts in U.S. History. Heather is a public historian and decolonial educator and travels
frequently to present on Indigenous history, including policy and activism. In the Munsee language,
Heather's name is Kiishookunkwe, meaning sunflower in full bloom.

CHAPTER 1

What Is Land Back?

Land Back is an Indigenous-led social movement that officially began in 2020. Its ideas, however, took root much earlier, as land rights have always been an important part of life for Indigenous nations. Land is a big part of Indigenous identity, and European colonization often violated land rights by taking Indigenous land by force. The United States has continued to take Indigenous lands in different ways over the years.

Indigenous people have never forgotten the land they came from. When they were being forced to leave, some chose to stay behind and fight for their land. Even after removal, many returned to fight for what had been taken from them. Some fought physical battles, while others fought legal battles in court.

Today, Indigenous people continue to work in many ways to regain rights to their homelands—by holding protests, raising money to buy land back, working to educate others and to pass laws, and filing court cases.

Indigenous relationships with the land are as important today as they were before Europeans arrived.

The term "Land Back" started as an internet meme in 2018, when Indigenous Canadians were protesting their government officials. Many disagreed with Prime Minister Justin Trudeau's policies and wanted control back over their lands. Arnell Tailfeathers of the Kainai Blood community was an internet personality who coined the term "Land Back."

The words quickly became a hashtag (#LandBack) and went viral. The simple message of Land Back helped to unite Indigenous organizers and activists alike, who were inspired to launch a movement. Indigenous youth around the world took up the term, and Indigenous artists created art that featured these words. Indigenous musicians even composed various songs called "Land Back."

The idea of Land Back gained traction and became wildly popular because it highlighted Indigenous people's deep connection to the land. Taking back their lands was about more than just property rights. It was about reclaiming Indigenous culture and ways of life, which are rooted in the land itself.

Indigenous peoples of Canada call themselves First Nations, First Peoples, or Aboriginal. In Mexico, Central America, and South America, Indigenous people use the Spanish terms *indígena* (Indigenous), *comunidad* (community), and *pueblo* (people). The issues Indigenous peoples face can be very different across these countries. But land loss, discrimination, and centuries of trauma have been experienced by most. In each case, though, Indigenous peoples have shown resilience. They are still here and ready to stand up for their rights and beliefs.

CHAPTER 2

Indigenous Relationship with Land

Indigenous people in the United States have always had a unique relationship with the land. It is a spiritual relationship, as the land is at the center of who Indigenous people are. Indigenous people see the land as something that is living and breathing. It is a part of them and they are a part of the land.

Over thousands of years, this relationship has strengthened. Indigenous people came to know the animals and plants of the lands in which they lived. Their culture and daily lives revolved around the land: through the crops they grew, the animals they hunted, or the houses they built.

Indigenous people practice a **sustainable** relationship with the land. They take only what is needed and replenish any resources that are taken. This connection is something that cannot be broken. Oral traditions within Indigenous communities tell how different nations came to be on the land, and how meaningful their relationship is with this land.

The sacredness of land and water has been at the core of much Indigenous activism.

This Ojibwe birchbark canoe is on display at Grand Portage National Monument in Minnesota, which is co-managed by the Grand Portage Band of Lake Superior Anishinaabe.

Indigenous nations around the Great Lakes region, for example, built winter and summer homes in different locations. Peoples like the Ojibwe tapped maple trees in early spring, and then boiled the sap down to create syrup and maple candies. They carved canoes from locally grown trees and fished from the lakes and rivers around their villages.

In 1796, an 80-year-old Oneida elder named Silversmith spoke of his devotion to the rocks and mountains. The Oneida are known as the "people of the standing stone." The Standing Stone represented their connection to the land.

Today, many Indigenous people are working to restore their own kinship with the land after centuries of removal. Many others continue Indigenous traditions that go back thousands of years.

However the world has changed, Indigenous beliefs offer comfort, resiliency, and belonging. These beliefs proclaim that the land knows who they are, and that they can see the land. The land is missed when Indigenous people are separated from it, but it also welcomes them home upon their return. The land never forgets Indigenous people.

"The Crow country is in exactly the right place. It has snowy mountains, sunny plains, all kinds of climates and good things for every season. When the summer heat scorches the prairies you can draw up under the mountains where the air is sweet and cool, the grass fresh, and the bright streams come tumbling out of the snow banks. . .

"In the autumn, when your horses are strong and fat from the mountain pastures, you can go down into the plains and hunt the buffalo or trap beaver in the streams. And when winter comes on you can take shelter in the woody bottoms along the rivers. . ."

—Crow Chief Eelápuash Speech to Rocky Mountain Fur Company, 1868

CHAPTER 3

Indigenous Land Loss

A home is more than just a building. It is also a place where you can feel calm, relaxed, and safe, a place that you know every inch of, and that is filled with memories of love, laughter, and sometimes even sorrow and loss. A home is also a place where you can dream and plan.

Losing a home is traumatic for anyone. Indigenous people often lost more than just their homes, though—they sometimes lost their entire homeland. Laws established made it mandatory for them to leave their homes, their villages, and the borders of their nations. The United States armed forces enforced those laws at gunpoint. Some nations were able to fight, and some fought for many years.

INDIAN LAND FOR SALE

GET A HOME
OF
YOUR OWN
❋
EASY PAYMENTS

PERFECT TITLE
❋
POSSESSION
WITHIN
THIRTY DAYS

FINE LANDS IN THE WEST

IRRIGATED IRRIGABLE **GRAZING** **AGRICULTURAL DRY FARMING**

IN 1910 THE DEPARTMENT OF THE INTERIOR SOLD UNDER SEALED BIDS ALLOTTED INDIAN LAND AS FOLLOWS:

Location.	Acres.	Average Price per Acre.	Location.	Acres.	Average Price per Acre.
Colorado	5,211.21	$7.27	Oklahoma	34,664.00	$19.14
Idaho	17,013.00	24.85	Oregon	1,020.00	15.43
Kansas	1,684.50	33.45	South Dakota	120,445.00	16.53
Montana	11,034.00	9.86	Washington	4,879.00	41.37
Nebraska	5,641.00	36.65	Wisconsin	1,069.00	17.00
North Dakota	22,610.70	9.93	Wyoming	865.00	20.64

FOR THE YEAR 1911 IT IS ESTIMATED THAT 350,000 ACRES WILL BE OFFERED FOR SALE

For information as to the character of the land write for booklet, "INDIAN LANDS FOR SALE," to the Superintendent U. S. Indian School at any one of the following places:

CALIFORNIA:
Hoopa.
COLORADO:
Ignacio.
IDAHO:
Lapwai.
KANSAS:
Horton.
Nadeau.

MINNESOTA:
Onigum.
MONTANA:
Crow Agency.
NEBRASKA:
Macy.
Santee.
Winnebago.

NORTH DAKOTA:
Fort Totten.
Fort Yates.
OKLAHOMA:
Anadarko.
Cantonment.
Colony.
Darlington.
Muskogee, DEPT. OF UNION AGENT.
Pawnee.

OKLAHOMA—Con.
Sac and Fox Agency.
Shawnee.
Wyandotte.
OREGON:
Klamath Agency.
Pendleton.
Roseburg.
Siletz.

SOUTH DAKOTA:
Cheyenne Agency.
Crow Creek.
Greenwood.
Lower Brule.
Pine Ridge.
Rosebud.
Sisseton.

WASHINGTON:
Fort Simcoe.
Fort Spokane.
Tekoa.
Tulalip.
WISCONSIN:
Oneida.

WALTER L. FISHER,
Secretary of the Interior.

ROBERT G. VALENTINE,
Commissioner of Indian Affairs.

The above ad came decades after the first sales of Indigenous land. In 1893, Indigenous land in Oklahoma was sold off to non-Indigenous settlers for as little as $1 per acre.

The first major removal policy was the Indian Removal Act of 1830. This act allowed the U.S. president to give lands west of the Mississippi River to eastern tribes willing to relocate. President Andrew Jackson used this policy to persuade, bribe, and threaten Indigenous peoples into signing removal treaties. Jackson signed almost 70 removal treaties, moving 50,000 Indigenous people off their ancestral land.

A large area of land where eastern Indigenous peoples settled was called Indian Territory. This land was originally home to the Wichita peoples, who were made up of Wichita, Waco, and Tawakoni peoples. The Wichita themselves were forced to move multiple times—first into Texas, then Oklahoma and Kansas. The reservation set aside for them in Oklahoma was taken away by the Confederate army during the Civil War. The Wichita fled north to Kansas, but they did not have land to farm there, and many people died of starvation and illness.

Tawakoni Jim was a chief of the Wichita peoples.

Even the reservations in Indian Territory did not remain under Indigenous control. In 1887, the General Allotment Act, also known as the Dawes Act, took reservation land and broke it up so that it was no longer held by Indigenous nations. Instead, small pieces of land were given to individual Indigenous people, but only those who registered. The rest of the land was sold to non-Indigenous settlers.

In 1954, the U.S. government began a policy of termination. This meant that the tribal status of Indigenous peoples would be terminated or ended. The policy also got rid of the reservation system. Following that, the 1956 Indian Relocation Act was passed to encourage Indigenous people to move off reservations and into big cities that needed labor. Many Indigenous people lost their homes due to this act and its enforcement, and for the most part, it brought them only further hardship and broken promises.

While many of these policies no longer exist today, the land that was taken and stolen was never returned. Treaties were broken, and Indigenous people were the ones who suffered. They were not allowed to go home. Those who did try to return found that their home had been forever changed.

Land Loss by the Numbers

- **98.9%** of Indigenous land has been lost since European colonization.

- More than **40%** of Indigenous nations now possess no federally recognized land.

- Only **2.3%** of the entire area of the United States is held in trust as federal Indigenous reservations.

- Today, there are **574** federally recognized Indigenous nations in the United States.

- **15** U.S. states–**30%**–have **0** federally recognized Indigenous nations due to removal policies.

CHAPTER 4

The 1868 Treaty of Fort Laramie

The Lakota and Dakota peoples lived and thrived for thousands of years in the Great Plains of central North America. As non-Indigenous settlers increasingly pushed westward, the Lakota and Dakota peoples fought to protect themselves and their homeland.

In 1868, these two Indigenous nations signed a treaty with the United States. The groups met at Fort Laramie, where they signed the Treaty of Fort Laramie. The terms of the treaty granted both these Indigenous nations full control of the Black Hills, which are a sacred place for Lakota people. Keeping political control of their holy sites was of utmost importance to them.

Articles of a Treaty made and concluded by and between Lieutenant General William T Sherman, General William S. Harney, General Alfred H Terry, General C.C Augur, S.D Henderson, Nathaniel G Taylor, John B Sanborn and Samuel F Tappan, duly appointed Commissioners on the part of the *United States* and the different Bands of the *Sioux Nation of Indians* by their Chiefs and Head men whose names are hereto subscribed; they being duly authorized to act in the premises

Article I   From this day forward all war between the parties to this agreement shall forever cease. The Government of the United States desires peace and its honor is hereby pledged to keep it. The Indians desire peace and they now pledge their honor to maintain it.

If bad men among the whites or among other people, subject to the authority of the United States, will commit any wrong upon the person or property of the Indians, the United States will, upon proof made to the Agent and forwarded to the Commissioner of Indian Affairs at Washington City, proceed at once to cause the offender to be arrested and punished according to the laws of the United States and also reimburse the injured person for the loss sustained

If bad men among the Indians shall commit a wrong or depredation upon the person or property of any one, white, black or Indian, subject to the authority of the United States and at peace therewith, the Indians herein named, solemnly agree that they

The original 1868 Treaty of Fort Laramie
is preserved in the National Archives.

The Treaty of Fort Laramie was ratified by the U.S. Senate, and it still stands as a legal document today. It should have been enforced as was intended, but non-Indigenous settlers did not honor the treaty. Gold was discovered in the Black Hills, and miners and settlers rushed in to acquire wealth. The U.S. government sent forces to protect the miners and settlers, and it ignored the terms of the treaty.

The Lakota and Dakota fought back to protect their homelands and to defend their rights. The fighting between the U.S. armed forces and the Lakota and Dakota peoples was fierce. Lakota heroes like Sitting Bull, Crazy Horse, and Red Cloud fought battles that struck the most brutal of blows to the U.S. Army. Among the most famous of these battles is the Battle of the Little Bighorn, where Lakota and Cheyenne warriors defeated Lieutenant Colonel George Armstrong Custer and his troops.

Sitting Bull was a Hunkpapa Lakota hero. He advocated for his people right up until his death at the hands of arresting officers.

The Lakota and Dakota people fought to protect the Black Hills.

The Lakota were not able to regain rights to the Black Hills. Instead, in 1927, parts of those hills were stripped and sculpted into Mount Rushmore. The mountain called Six Grandfathers, a holy site for the Lakota, now bears the faces of four U.S. presidents. Mount Rushmore opened in 1941 and, for over 80 years, those faces have added both insult and injury to the Indigenous nations who lived on, loved, and cared for those hills for thousands of years.

In 1980, the Supreme Court agreed with the Lakota, ruling that the Black Hills had been illegally taken from them. It ordered the U.S. government to pay the Lakota for the land. The Lakota refused the settlement and are still refusing it today because they do not want money. They simply want their land back.

Men pose in 1892 among mountains of bison skulls.

The U.S. armed forces protected settlers and worked to drive Indigenous people away. Because the Indigenous way of life centered so strongly on bison in the Great Plains, U.S. officials worked to kill as many bison as possible. Millions of bison were killed, destroying an important Indigenous food source. Plains tribes have a spiritual kinship with the bison, too, that is part of their history, culture, and religious practices. As such, the destruction of the bison left them grief-stricken and in mourning. U.S. officials had hoped to demoralize Indigenous warriors and to break their spirit with this slaughter, but they failed.

CHAPTER 5

The Land Back Movement

In July 2020, former President Donald Trump scheduled a campaign rally at Mount Rushmore. Lakota activists protested and blocked the road to Mount Rushmore. These activists were called Land Defenders, and they were part of the NDN Collective, an Indigenous-led rights organization. The NDN Collective created a **manifesto** that outlined the goals of the Land Back movement. It was titled "The Reclamation of Everything Stolen from the Original Peoples," and it includes 13 organizing principles.

One of Land Back's main goals is to close Mount Rushmore in South Dakota. The movement wants the land returned to the Lakota people. But the movement is about more than just that one place. It stands for all places that once belonged to Indigenous people. It is about recognizing Indigenous rights and Indigenous **stewardship**.

Lakota activists protested the rally held beneath Mount Rushmore in July 2020.

There are four goals that are central to the Land Back movement. The first involves dismantling White supremacy structures that keep Indigenous people oppressed. The second speaks to defunding systems that enforce oppression and disconnecting those

systems from stewardship of the land. The third demands the return of all public lands to Indigenous people. The fourth calls for movement into a new policy era around free and informed consent.

The South Dakota National Guard removed protesters to make way for former president Donald Trump's rally. Twenty-one protesters were arrested.

Land Back has become a political statement as well as a strong reminder of what is at stake.

Across the United States, land is being returned to Indigenous nations. The return of all this public, private, and state land ensures that wrongs are righted and that the Indigenous connection to the land is restored. Some of these success stories include land set aside for the Mashpee Wampanoag in Massachusetts. The Wampanoag people are those who first met the Pilgrims who sailed on the *Mayflower* in 1620. Another newsworthy success was the return of a Californian island to the Wiyot people.

Over 2 square miles (5 square kilometers) of land in this Minnesota state park are being returned to the Upper Sioux Community whose ancestors died there after federal officers withheld rations.

Wyandotte, Passamaquoddy, Ojibwe, and Esselen people have also succeeded in reclaiming large areas of ancestral land through negotiation and land purchases. These various efforts seek to heal centuries of loss, trauma, and injustice. While there is still much to be done to achieve equity and justice, the Land Back movement is helping by taking the first steps forward.

Indigenous activists rallied for justice in 2020 and set a movement into motion.

Land Back 13 Organizing Principles

1. Don't burn bridges: Even when there is conflict between groups or organizers remember that we are fighting for all of our peoples and we will continue to be in community even after this battle

2. Don't defend our ways

3. Organize to win

4. Move from abundance—We come from a space of scarcity. We must work from a place of abundance

5. We bring our people with us

6. Deep relationships by attraction, not promotion

7. Divest/invest

8. We value our warriors

9. Room for grace—be able to be human

10. We cannot let our oppressors' inhumanity take away from ours

11. Strategy includes guidance

12. Realness: Sometimes the truth hurts

13. Unapologetic but keep it classy

— from the Landback Manifesto and the NDN Collective

EXTEND YOUR LEARNING

BOOKS

Higgins, Nadia. *Defending the Land: Causes and Effects of Red Cloud's War.* Capstone Press, Mankato, MN, 2015.

Loh-Hagan, Virgina. *Stand Up, Speak Out: Indigenous Rights.* 45th Parallel Press, Ann Arbor, MI, 2022.

Schwartz, Heather E. *Forced Removal: Cause and Effects of the Trail of Tears.* Capstone Press, Mankato, MN, 2015.

Sorell, Traci. *We Are Still Here! Native American Truths Everyone Should Know.* Charlesbridge, Watertown, MA, 2021.

WEBSITES

With an adult, learn more online with these suggested searches.

"Land Back: The Indigenous Fight to Reclaim Lands (Above the Noise)," PBS Learning Media.

"National Museum of the American Indian," Smithsonian.

"The Future for Native Americans," Library of Congress.

GLOSSARY

abundance (uh-BUHN-duhns) having much

activists (AK-ti-vists) people who take action for political purposes

ancestral (an-SE-struhl) belongs to a person through inheritance

colonization (kah-luh-nuh-ZAY-shuhn) the building of settlements on land belonging to others in order to increase a nation's power and/or wealth; often accomplished by armed force

consent (kuhn-SENT) explicit approval or agreement

enforced (in-forsd) carried out by force

kinship (KIN-ship) relationship

manifesto (ma-nuh-FE-stoh) written statement of motivations

meme (MEEM) an entertaining item spread online

resilience (ri-ZIL-yuhns) ability to recover and persevere despite hardship

social movement (SOH-shuhl MOOV-muhnt) a campaign in support of changing society's values

stewardship (STOO-uhrd-ship) the responsibility to care for something

sustainable (suh-STAY-nuh-buhl) suitable for long-term usage

violated (VIE-uh-lay-ted) wronged

INDEX